Restorative justice: the art of an emancipated crime approach

Restorative justice:
the art of an emancipated crime approach

Inaugural address
Delivered by Dr Jacques Claessen
upon the acceptance
of his office as
endowed professor of
restorative justice
at Maastricht University
on 4 November 2022

eleven

Published, sold and distributed by Eleven
P.O. Box 85576
2508 CG The Hague
The Netherlands
Tel.: +31 70 33 070 33
Fax: +31 70 33 070 30
e-mail: sales@elevenpub.nl
www.elevenpub.com

Sold and distributed in USA and Canada
Independent Publishers Group
814 N. Franklin Street
Chicago, IL 60610, USA
Order Placement: +1 800 888 4741
Fax: +1 312 337 5985
orders@ipgbook.com
www.ipgbook.com

Eleven is an imprint of Boom uitgevers Den Haag.

ISBN 978-94-6236-519-3
ISBN 978-94-0011-246-9 (E-book)

© 2023 Jacques Claessen | Eleven

'For everything that lives is holy.'
William Blake[1]

'Do not do to another what you do not wish
to happen to you. Do unto others, at all times,
as much good as you in equal circumstances
would wish to receive from them.'
*Article 6 of the Dutch State Regulations
for the Batavian People 1798*[2]

---

1   W. Blake, *Het huwelijk van hemel en hel*, Utrecht: Erven J. Bijleveld, 2001, p. 123.
2   J. Rosendaal, *Staatsregeling voor het Bataafsche volk 1798. De eerste grondwet van Nederland*, Nijmegen: Vantilt, 2005, p. 60.

Dear Rector Magnificus, dear colleagues and students, dear family and friends, esteemed people here in the hall and via the livestream elsewhere,

Always treat every human being well

More than ten years ago, I was also in this place. Then, in the context of my promotion to doctor. Now, because of my inauguration as endowed professor of restorative justice. Back then, I concluded my 'PhD-talk' with the following words of Lao Tse, a Chinese philosopher from the sixth century BC: 'Treat those who are good with goodness, and also treat those who are not good with goodness. Thus goodness is attained.'[3] The question is whether there are good and bad people. In my view, there aren't. Every human being is potentially capable of everything, including behaviour that we call good as well as behaviour that we call bad. Furthermore, no human being performs only good or bad acts, while every human being is constantly changing. Moreover, 'good' and 'bad' are to some extent relative and fluid concepts. So, in my view, there are no bad people, only people who are damaged and confused by internal and/or external factors and who can do – and sometimes actually do – bad things.[4] Nevertheless, I still find Lao Tse's words very apt. After all, what he wants to say is that even people who behave badly should be treated well. I read in his words the instruction to mankind not to harm their fellow human begins, when they have committed an evil or a wrong deed – in my view: not to harm them even more. In fact, Lao Tse's instruction to mankind is to help their fellow human beings who have committed a wrongdoing. After all, doing good goes beyond mere not harming.

---

3   H.D.T. Rost, *The Golden Rule. A Universal Ethic*, Oxford: George Ronald, 1986, p. 43 and 162.

4   B. Katie & S. Mitchell, *Duizend namen voor vreugde*, Amsterdam: Forum, 2007, p. 73, 94 and 161.

We find the same message with Plato. In his work on the State, this Greek philosopher from the fourth century BC lets his teacher Socrates discuss the question of what constitutes good behaviour with someone called Polemarchos. He holds the view that a person behaves well when they give others what they deserve, which, according to Polemarchos, means owing positive things to friends. When Socrates then asks him about enemies, he replies: 'What you owe an enemy is what an enemy deserves: something negative.' But, Socrates continues, don't people just get worse when they are treated badly by other people? And doesn't a worse person just become worse behaved? Polemarchos answers both questions in the affirmative. But '[h]ow can a good action ever produce bad results?', Socrates asks. Polemarchos – by now out of sorts – agrees that good behaviour can never result in a person becoming worse and behaving worse. Plato lets Socrates conclude as follows:

> 'We therefore conclude that a person does not behave well if, as a result of his behaviour, another person suffers badly, even if that other person is an enemy. (...) So if someone says that good behaviour means treating one's fellow human beings according to what they deserve, and if for him this then means that a man ought to treat his enemies badly, he thereby shows a lack of insight, for we observe that it can never be good to treat anyone badly.'[5]

---

5   Plato, *De ideale staat. Politeia*, Amsterdam: Athenaeum-Polak & Van Gennep, 2005, p. 22.

The message that every human being should always be treated well is also found in the Bible, when Jesus says to his pupils:

> 'You have heard that it was said, you must love your neighbour and hate your enemy. But I say to you: Love your enemies; (...) do good to those who hate you; (...) so that you may be children of your father, who is in the heavens, for he makes his sun rise on good and bad people, and makes it rain on the righteous and the unrighteous.'[6]

The Golden Rule

Well regarded, Lao Tse, Plato and Jesus plead for a life that is lived according to the Golden Rule. Formulated negatively, this rule implies: 'Do not do to another what you do not want others to do to you.' Formulated positively, it implies: 'Treat another as you would like to be treated yourself.'[7] The Golden Rule corresponds to the moral guideline of the German philosopher Arthur Schopenhauer: 'Harm no one; on the contrary, help everyone, as much as you can.'[8] Besides, the things you do have to do with *why* you do them.[9] Lao Tse explicitly shows that what you do – namely, always treat every human being well – is related to the reason why you do it, when he says: 'Thus goodness is attained.' Living by the Golden Rule leads to a society that is good or just and peaceful.

6   Gospel according to Matthew 5:43-45 (Sermon on the Mount).
7   On the Golden Rule, see among others: K. Amstrong, *De heilige natuur. Hoe we de relatie met onze natuurlijke omgeving kunnen herstellen*, Amsterdam/Antwerpen: Het Getij/Querido Facto, 2022, especially chapter 8.
8   A. Schopenhauer, *Dat ben jij. Over de grondslag van de moraal*, Amsterdam: Wereldbibliotheek, 2010, p. 120 and 138.
9   W. Hart, *Anders vasthouden. 9 sleutels voor het werken vanuit de bedoeling*, Amsterdam: Boom, 2020, p. 23-42.

In his book on the Golden Rule, the American philosopher Rost shows that it is a universal moral rule; in fact, it can be found in all known religions and philosophies of life. Interestingly, Rost relates the Golden Rule to the also universal principle of reciprocity and distinguishes between different levels. At the lowest level is the Iron Rule, which stands for 'an eye for an eye, a tooth for a tooth'. This rule prohibits disproportionate retaliation, but legitimises proportional retaliation, or retribution of evil with evil. Then comes the Iron Rule with a thin veneer of gold, where the response to a crime takes into account not only a person's behaviour, but also their state of mind, intention and motives. This rule is followed by the Silver Rule and the Golden Rule, with the Silver Rule being the negatively formulated Golden Rule: 'Do not do to another what you do not want others to do to you.' The Golden Rule is positively formulated and, as mentioned, implies: 'Treat another as you would like to be treated yourself.' The highest expression of the Golden Rule overlaps with the 'rule' that goes beyond the principle of reciprocity, namely: the 'Rule' of Love (*agapè*).[10] Indeed, even when someone does not treat you well, the Golden Rule instructs you to treat that other human being well. Starting from the retribution of evil with evil based on the Iron Rule, we have now arrived at the retribution of evil with good based on the Golden Rule.

---

10 Rost 1986, p. 9 and 65-67. See on *agapè*: C. van den Broeke, *Heb uw naaste niet lief als uzelf? De rol van naastenliefde in het recht, de rechtstheologie en het kerkrecht*, Kampen: Theologische Universiteit Kampen, 2021, p. 25: 'Through *agapè*, a person tries to do justice to another person, to cooperate in the improvement of the other person's position, to interpret the voice of the other person, to bring redemption to the other person who is stuck, to put the other person in his or her power.'

The view of mankind and the world behind the Golden Rule

And that – the retribution of evil with good – is quite a task, especially when someone has committed a serious crime. Rost therefore argues that observing the Golden Rule requires 'an undefeatable attitude of goodwill' that stems from the belief that 'no man is an island' and that 'all human beings are one family'.[11] This conviction actually concerns the view of mankind and the world behind the Golden Rule. This view is closely related to what the recently deceased Buddhist Zen teacher Thich Nhat Hanh calls 'interbeing'.[12] This concept, which Thich Nhat Hanh explains using the Heart Sutra – an important Buddhist scripture – implies that everything, including every human being, is empty of an isolated, separated self. At the same time, everything, including every human being, is full of everything in the universe. In Thich Nhat Hanh's own words: 'We do not stand on our own. We are inextricably connected. (...) Everything contains everything else; that is the principle of permeating each other. (...) [T]he wave (...) realizes that it is only water, that there is only water.'[13] The concept of interbeing can be related to the so-called Net of Indra – an image that is central in another Buddhist scripture, namely the Flower Ornament Sutra.[14] In the abode of the God Indra hangs a miraculous net that extends into infinity on all sides. At every junction of the net hangs a unique sparkling jewel. Because the net is immeasurable, the number of jewels is innumerable. Looking at any jewel, you can see that in its shiny surface all

---

11   Rost 1986, p. 67, 79 and 165.
12   Thich Nhat Hanh, *Vorm is leegte, leegte is vorm. Commentaar op de Prajna-paramita hartsoetra*, Rotterdam: Asoka, 2005, p. 15 and 19. See in this context also: K. Nishida, *An Inquiry into the Good*, New Haven/London: Yale University Press, 1990, especially p. 19: 'It is not that there is experience because there is an individual, but that there is an individual because there is experience. The individual's experience is simply a small, distinctive sphere of limited experience within true experience.'
13   Thich Nhat Hanh, 2005, p. 45, 47 and 53.
14   See: www.zenamsterdam.nl/nl/maarten-bode-over-de-avatamsakasoetra.

other jewels are reflected – to infinity. The jewels stand for human beings, animals, plants, things – for all that is. Indra's Net shows that everything is connected and interpermeated. This image portrays existence as 'a vast web of interdependencies in which, if one thread is disturbed, the whole web is shaken'.[15] The focus is not on 'distinct, separate entities', but on 'the relationships between these same entities':[16] 'To be is to be related.'[17] And this means that to do evil upon others is to do evil upon yourself and to harm others is to harm yourself,[18] for I am you and you are me.[19] When the illusion of separateness gives way to the insight of relatedness, it is no longer the retribution of evil with evil based on the Iron Rule that is natural and obvious, but rather the retribution of evil with good based on the Golden Rule.[20]

Spiritual awakening and spiritual maturing

As mentioned, Rost argues that adherence to the Golden Rule stems from the belief that 'no man is an island' and that 'all human beings are one family'. The American philosopher David Loy goes a step further by arguing that adherence to the Golden Rule actually requires a

---

15 F.H. Cook, *Hua-yen Buddhism. The Jewel Net of Indra*, University Park/London: The Pennsylvania State University Press, 1977, p. 1. See also: T. Lathouwers, *Zij is altijd soms. Vrouwelijke gestalten van compassie*, Rotterdam: Asoka, 2019, p. 173 and 201.

16 Cook 1977, p. 8.

17 W. Wielemans, *Voorbij het individu. Mensbeelden in wetenschappen*, Leuven/ Apeldoorn: Garant, 1993, p. 1. See also: C. Lu, *De Boeddha in de bajes*, Amsterdam: Spectrum, 2019, especially p. 41, 50-51, 65, 86-87, 101 and 123. The view that people are 'junctions of relationships' is also central to the so-called process philosophy, of which the British-American philosopher Alfred North Whitehead is considered the founder. See in this context: C. Robert Mesle, *Process-Relational Philosophy. An Introduction to Alfred North Whitehead*, West Conshohocken: Templeton Press, 2008.

18 Armstrong 2022, p. 186.

19 Lu 2019, p. 41.

20 See on 'the illusion of separateness' and 'the insight of connectedness': Schopenhauer 2010, p. 171-186.

person to *experience* being one with another person; experiencing is different from believing.[21] According to Loy, meditation can help in experiencing the so-called non-duality of me and the other.[22] Within this context, it is important to reflect on the distinction between spiritual *awakening* and spiritual *maturing*, as made by the American philosopher Ken Wilber. Spiritual awakening has to do with *what* a person sees. It is about experiencing – with the help of meditation – the non-duality of me and the other. However, a full spiritual life also requires spiritual maturing. Becoming spiritually mature has to do with *how* someone sees something, which interpretation and meaning he gives to what he sees. The latter depends on his worldview – and worldviews evolve. For now, that evolution looks as follows: from magical to mythical, from mythical to modern-rational, from modern-rational to postmodern-pluralistic and from postmodern-pluralistic to integral. While the magical worldview is egocentric and the mythical is ethnocentric in nature, the rational and pluralistic worldviews are world-centric in nature. And while the rational worldview focuses on classifying and critically analyzing different perspectives,[23] the pluralist worldview is characterized by the equal coexistence of a multitude of perspectives.[24] The point to which evolution has taken us so far is the integral worldview, with the understanding that it is not currently prevalent. About this worldview, Wilber says: 'The integral worldview sees itself as inseparable from the whole universe. This is a Cosmos in which

---

21 D. Loy, 'Indra's Postmodern Net', *Philosophy East & West* 1993, 3, p. 481-510, p. 484.

22 Loy 1993, p. 503. See also: Cook 1977, p. 120-121; P. van der Sterren, *Over het brein, non-dualiteit en vrije wil*, Amsterdam: Samsara, 2013.

23 See also: A. Lacroix, *Hoe word je geen slaaf van het systeem?*, Utrecht: Ten Have, 2021, p. 14.

24 K. Wilber, *Integrale wijsheid en de toekomst van de spiritualiteit*, Amsterdam: Samsara, 2018, p. 89; K. Wilber, *Integrale meditatie. Mindfulness als pad naar Opgroeien, Ontwaken en Openstaan*, Amsterdam: Samsara, 2019.

everything is seamlessly connected (...). [T]he integral worldview [is] truly holistic.'[25] This worldview involves the integration of different perspectives, where not reason but intuition is central.[26] Moreover, it is not until mankind reaches this 'level' that they become persons who 'live' the world-centred perspective rather than merely profess it with their mouth, according to Wilber.[27] In short: becoming spiritually awake and mature is necessary to arrive at the insight of *universal* connectedness as well as the *universal* practice of the Golden Rule.

Restorative justice as a spiritually mature or emancipated approach to crime

Scholars who have applied Wilber's thinking to criminal law and criminology argue that it is only from the integral worldview that a space emerges in which the 'protection of society can be reconciled with reducing the suffering of those who are in need of some form of external control or intervention' – i.e. people who commit crime.[28] In doing so, they explicitly point to restorative justice to arrive at this reconciliation.[29] In sum, they are saying that with the advent of restorative justice in criminal justice and criminology, the approach to crime is becoming spiritually mature. Equally, one can speak of the emergence of an emancipated approach to crime, now that 'emancipation' originally stands for the process of maturing. What these scholars are also implicitly saying is that the insight of connectedness, the Golden Rule and restorative justice have something to do with each other. I will pay attention to this connection at several points in my inaugural address.

---

25 Wilber 2018, p. 92.
26 See also: Lacroix 2021, p. 33.
27 Cited in: J.J. Gibbs, D. Giever & K.A. Pober, 'Criminology and the Eye of the Spirit', *Journal of Contemporary Criminal Justice* 2000, February, p. 99-127, p. 116.
28 Gibbs, Giever & Pober 2000, p. 121.
29 Gibbs, Giever & Pober 2000, p. 121.

Restorative justice: a definition

But first: what is restorative justice? Restorative justice can be defined as 'a theory of justice that emphasizes repairing the harm caused by criminal behaviour, which is best accomplished through cooperative processes that allow all willing stakeholders to meet, although other approaches are available when that is impossible'.[30] It follows from this definition that restorative justice – like criminal justice – is a theory of justice, which answers the question of what should be done when a crime has been committed. According to this theory of justice, the aim of the response to crime should be restoration of the harm caused. This should include material and immaterial damage as well as relational and moral damage. The path by which the restoration of harm should take place, ideally consists of cooperative processes in which as many parties as possible are actively involved on a voluntary basis. This could include the offender, the victim, their family and friends, other members of the community as well as public authorities. What is important about this definition is that – when cooperative processes prove impossible – it allows for other approaches, as long as the restoration of harm is the goal.

Restorative justice and the Golden Rule

Restorative justice and the Golden Rule agree – negatively formulated – that there is no room for punishment in the sense of the intentional infliction of suffering or pain in order to retaliate or to take proportionate revenge. After all, by retaliating or taking proportionate revenge, harm is inflicted on the offender intentionally. The offender is deliberately treated badly. Harm is inflicted on them

---

30 See: www.restorativejustice.org. For other definitions, see among others: J. Claessen & K. Roelofs, 'Herstelrecht(voorzieningen) en mediation in strafzaken', in: J. Boksem, P. Mevis, D. Paridaens, C. Waling & H. Wolswijk (red.), *Handboek strafzaken*, Deventer: Wolters Kluwer 2020, chapter 49 (online).

wilfully. As far as distributive justice is concerned, both restorative justice and the Golden Rule at least imply the refusal to harm another human being – even when that other human being has committed a crime. Stated positively, restorative justice is an approach to crime that is aimed at restoring the harm suffered, as well as – at least in my view – at preventing new harm, namely by restoring harm suffered in a sustainable way as well as by removing the causes that led to this harm. In short: not retribution of harm with harm, but restoration and prevention of harm are central to restorative justice. Do restorative justice and the Golden Rule also correspond in positive terms? Specifically, does an approach to crime that focuses on restoration and prevention of harm also do justice to the task of treating others well? Since restoration and prevention of harm take place in a humane manner in restorative justice, this is, in my view, by all means the case.

Restoration as reverse retribution

As a rule, restoration – like punishment – does involve suffering for the offender. However, while punishment can be defined as the intentional addition of suffering, the suffering associated with restoration is not a goal in itself, but an almost inevitable side effect – after all, restoration costs effort, time, money *et cetera*. Just as the Belgian criminologist Lode Walgrave, I consider restoration to be *reverse* retribution:[31] the offender does not deserve harm because of their crime, but they bear the responsibility to repair the harm

---

31 L. Walgrave, *Being consequential about restorative justice*, Den Haag: Eleven, 2021; J. Claessen, 'Pleidooi voor en uitwerking van een maximalistisch herstelrecht', *Tijdschrift voor Herstelrecht* 2020, 4, p. 18-30; J. Claessen, 'Pleidooi voor de terugdringing van de korte gevangenisstraf', *Tijdschrift voor Strafrecht* 2021, 3, p. 131-137; J. Claessen, 'Pleidooi voor de (door)ontwikkeling van de taakstraf en thuisdetentie ter vervanging van de korte gevangenisstraf', *Tijdschrift voor Strafrecht* 2022, 1, p. 6-12.

they have caused the victim and/or the community with his crime.[32]
Sometimes restoration is literally possible. More often, restoration
will be partly or entirely symbolic in nature. Consider for example
offenders acknowledging their crimes, making apologies and pay-
ing compensation.

The importance of self-restoration

Restorative justice is not exclusively about the restoration between
the offender and the victim and/or the community. Equally important are the restoration of the offender (self-restoration) as well as
the restoration between the offender and their social network – i.e.
their family, relatives and friends. Without working on these forms
of restoration first, achieving restoration between the offender, the
victim and/or the community may not even be possible. An important part of treating the offender well – on top of not harming them
further – is to enable and encourage their resocialisation and reha-
bilitation. In other words: the pre-existing damage to the offender
that – in part – led to their crime as well as the new damage caused
to themselves by their crime should be repaired, while the causes
of this damage should be removed as much as possible. This self-
restoration of the offender can provide the space within the offender
necessary to make a positive contribution to the realization of their
restoration towards the victim and/or the community. Moreover, the
offender's self-restoration may prevent further victims.

---

32 See also: H. Bianchi, *Ethiek van het straffen*, Nijkerk: G.F. Callenbach, 1964,
    p. 64-77; H. Bianchi, *Gerechtigheid als vrijplaats. De terugkeer van het slachtoffer
    in ons recht*, Baarn: Ten Have, 1985, p. 31-34. Bianchi points out that retribu-
    tion originally had the meaning of 'an eye for *the compensation of* an eye and a
    tooth for *the compensation of* a tooth'. In short: reparation matches the origi-
    nal meaning of retribution.

Maximalist restorative justice: focus on the goal of restoration

Although restorative justice thinkers prefer cooperative processes, in which as many parties as possible are actively involved on a voluntary basis, maximalist restorative justice thinkers, to whom Walgrave and I belong, also advocate other approaches aimed at the restoration of harm when cooperative processes prove impossible. In criminal law, this could include prioritizing sanctions with a strong restorative component over sanctions with a large retributive component. Concretely: in the context of sanctioning, the Public Prosecutor or the judge then prioritizes community service over imprisonment as much as possible. From a maximalist restorative justice approach, there is only room for deprivation of liberty if an offender poses a serious danger to society and that danger cannot be curbed in any other way – not even by extensive restriction of liberty, such as electronic home detention. When deprivation of liberty proves unavoidable, much effort should be put into restoration within the context of detention. Ideally, both regular detention and electronic home detention create a 'sanctuary' in and from which restoration is being worked on: restoration of the offender himself, restoration between the offender and their social network, restoration between the offender and the victim and restoration between the offender and the community. Because there is no room for retribution in a maximalist restorative justice approach, confinement takes on the character of a (treatment) measure rather than a punishment.[33] As many as over eighty per cent of all prisoners in the Netherlands are imprisoned for less than six months. The multi-year national change programme *Changing Justice Gears*, of which I have been one of the coordinators since 2020, looks at reducing this short-term detention. We seek to achieve this goal, for example, by putting into practice a

---

33 H. Jongeneel & J. Claessen, 'Naar een gevangenisstraf met behandeling', *Nederlands Juristenblad* 2018, p. 1364-1367.

number of maximalist restorative justice ideas, including prioritising restoration and resocialisation over retribution and deterrence as sanction goals, as well as – by extension – prioritising community service and electronic home detention – ideally in restorative form – over regular detention.[34]

Distributive as well as procedural justice

Maximalist restorative justice focuses on distributive justice, on the intended purpose of restorative justice, namely restoration and prevention of harm. 'Perfect' restorative justice – and, according to minimalist restorative justice thinkers, the only true restorative justice – also focuses on procedural justice, on the path by which the intended goal is achieved. As mentioned, restoration ideally takes place through cooperative processes, in which as many parties as possible are actively involved on a voluntary basis. Restorative justice-thinkers want to return the conflict – even if it underlies crime or arises from crime – as much as possible to the original parties. After all, the conflict is their 'property' – in the words of the Norwegian criminologist Nils Christie.[35] It is strange that a conflict, as soon as it has to do with crime, should be taken away by the state – especially from the victim and the community, who are represented by the Public Prosecutor in criminal law, but who are, unlike the accused, not themselves full parties to the proceedings. Invariably, we read in the literature on criminal law that this 'expropriation' is done to prevent someone 'taking the law into their own hands'.[36] The idea is that, if the approach to crime were left to the citizens

---

34 J. Claessen & S. Meijer, 'Het project *Changing Justice Gears* en de terugdringing van de korte gevangenisstraf', *Sancties* 2022, 5, p. 288-299.
35 N. Christie, 'Conflicts as Property', *British Journal of Criminology* 1977, 1, p. 1-15.
36 C. Kelk & F. de Jong, *Studieboek materieel strafrecht*, Deventer: Wolters Kluwer, 2019, p. 1; N. Jörg, C. Kelk & A. Klip, *Strafrecht met mate*, Deventer: Wolters Kluwer, 2019, p. 1.

themselves, it would inevitably lead to disproportionate retaliation – something that even goes against the Iron Rule, 'an eye for an eye, a tooth for a tooth'.

In that context, reference is often made to the way in which crime was dealt with before the Modern Era, when there was no criminal law as we know it today. However, historical research shows that many crimes at that time were handled relatively peacefully by the conflicting parties themselves – under the guidance of secular and/or religious authorities: the conflicting parties discussed what had happened and negotiated compensation. Anthropological research shows that this approach to crime still exists in cultures which the Modern Era has passed by. I have experienced this first hand in the inlands of Suriname during a research on the traditional conflict resolution among the Indigenous people and the Maroons.[37] Many restorative justice-thinkers are inspired by the crime approach as it exists among Aborigines in Australia, Māori in New Zealand and Indigenous people in the America's. But let it be clear: by no means all aspects of this approach are useful in the context of a contemporary crime approach. As far as the Indigenous people and the Maroons in Suriname are concerned, think, for instance, of 'beating' as a means of exerting pressure on denying suspects or corporal punishment for offenders of serious crimes. The art is to reconcile the best of the pre-modern crime approach with the best of the modern crime approach – something for which there is room seen from the integral worldview.[38]

---

37 J. Claessen & R. Djokarto, 'Conflictbeslechting na misdaad bij de Marrons in Suriname. Mogelijke bruggen tussen de traditionele en moderne misdaad-aanpak', *Tijdschrift voor Herstelrecht* 2020, 2, p. 60-79. See also: E.A. Hoebel, *The Law of Primitive Man. A Study in Comparative Legal Dynamics*, Cambridge/London: Harvard University Press, 1954.

38 This wordview also creates space to apply the best of the pre-modern crime approach not only within one's own community, but *universally*.

Even though I am a maximalist restorative justice thinker, together with my puristic colleagues I recognize that our modern crime approach is not only distributively, but also procedurally inadequate. The modern criminal process is a vertical process between the government and the lawyer of the accused in particular. The focus lies on finding the 'material truth' and – in case of sufficient evidence – the top-down determination of the attached 'price tag' for the offender. In my view, this is a cold, business-like way of doing justice – a way that leaves the underlying conflict between people unaltered. The latter is not surprising, since in criminal law a crime is primarily seen as a violation of the legal order, which should be restored through punishment. In restorative justice however, a crime is first and foremost seen as an interpersonal conflict, as a violation of people and their relationships. Unlike criminal justice, restorative justice is not about abstract pacification of the legal order, but about concrete conflict resolution between people. While reconciliation between conflicting parties is not always possible, restorative justice at least aims at some neutralization of the underlying conflict. And this requires more horizontalization and democratization than is seen in the vertical, paternalistic criminal process.

Mediation as an important restorative justice provision

One important restorative justice provision is mediation.[39] Last summer, I attended a mediation training on Curaçao. There – in a nutshell – I learned the following. Mediation is a process that, unlike a legal process, aims to create a win-win situation. This win-win situation becomes possible, among other things, because the mediator – actively listening to the stories of the parties – pays attention to the destructive communication between and the negative emotions of

---

39 A. Brenninkmeijer et al., *Handboek mediation*, Den Haag: Sdu, 2017.

the parties. In this context, it is important to realize that behind every reproach and negative emotion, there is an unmet need. Initially (the first half of the process), mediation is primarily a sociopsychological process in which the focus is on active listening, improving communication, channelling emotions and uncovering unmet needs. When parties manage to touch each other with their own Greek tragedy and thus with their vulnerability as human beings, an opening usually arises. During mediation in criminal cases, the offender – by listening to the victim's story – can start to see the harm they have done with their crime.[40] Seeing the victim's suffering can help the offender break open their armour, which prevents them from feeling their own pain as well as that of others.[41] Incidentally, this can also happen the other way round. Furthermore, during mediation in criminal cases, the victim can – by listening to the offender's story – come to realize that the offender is not a monster or a devil, but like themselves a vulnerable and damaged human being. Once the air between the parties has cleared (concretely: when the relational and moral harm has been restored), the viewpoints previously held by the parties are often abandoned. A viewpoint is a possible answer to an unmet need. For example, the victim's viewpoint that the offender deserves a severe punishment and/or has to pay high compensation. During a mediation, it can 'just' happen that the anger-fuelled destructive viewpoint 'The offender must suffer for this!' gives way to the more open and constructive viewpoint 'Something must be

---

40 In this regard, see: J. Jonas-van Dijk, S. Zebel, J. Claessen & H. Nelen, 'The Psychological Impact of Participation in Victim-Offender Mediation on Offenders: Evidence for Increased Compunction and Victim Empathy', *Frontiers in Psychology* 2022, 12, p. 1-13; J. Jonas-van Dijk, S. Zebel, J. Claessen & H. Nelen, 'Victim-Offender Mediation and Reduced Reoffending: Gauging the Self-Selection Bias', *Crime & Delinquency* 2020, 6-7, p. 949-972.
41 Lu 2019, p. 117-118.

done about this!'[42] More answers suddenly turn out to be possible in response to unmet needs. It is virtually always about the parties' needs to be recognized and seen as human beings. So too in mediation in criminal cases. By committing their crime, the offender has trampled on this need of the victim. During mediation, the offender can rectify this by taking responsibility for what they have done. They may confess, repent and apologize. However, the offender too has the need to be recognized and seen as a human being who is more than their crime. Mediation offers scope for this aspect as well. For example, the victim can willingly accept the offender's confession, remorse and apology. They can also show understanding for the offender's side of the story. During the remainder of the mediation (the second half of the process), the parties can negotiate and agree freely and creatively on 'how to proceed?' and 'what is needed to achieve this?'.

Restorative justice provisions in general

There are of course parallels between mediation and restorative justice provisions in general. Narratives, emotions and needs, for example, also play an important role in the context of other restorative justice provisions. These also take centre stage in restorative conferences, which are not only attended by the offender and the victim, but also by their family and friends and the larger community.[43] It is precisely because of this focus on narratives, emotions and needs that restorative justice is, in my view, a warm, humane way of doing

---

42 J. Claessen, 'Martha Nussbaums *Anger and Forgiveness*. Over vergelding en vergeving en over woede en liefde', *Tijdschrift voor Herstelrecht* 2018, 3, p. 14-32; J. Claessen, 'Johan en het vuur – reflectie: *ira* (woede)', in: M. Sanders (red.), *Voor God kom ik mijn cel uit. Verhalen uit een jeugdgevangenis*, Heeswijk-Dinther: Berne Media, 2022, p. 103-108.

43 See issue 3 of the *Tijdschrift voor Herstelrecht* 2022, which is entirely devoted to (the added value of) conferencing.

justice. People and their social environment are paramount – not the systemic world of the law, although restorative justice does not escape a certain degree of legalization either.[44] During a mediation or restorative conference, empathy, understanding and compassion can emerge on both sides alongside positive changes in awareness, perception and attitude.[45] Ideally, a person-to-person encounter takes place. This encounter first and foremost requires an open and curious attitude towards the other person – and, all things considered, also towards oneself, since through the contact with other people, one also gets to know oneself better. More than that even: a person changes through meeting others.[46] The French philosopher Charles Pépin argues that an encounter can give rise to 'a shock creating cracks in our shield', causing 'a wind of freedom [to start blowing] through a rigid identity'.[47] Face to face with the other, we break free from our egocentricity and experience our responsibility towards the other.[48] One could say: the illusion of separateness gives way to the insight of connectedness including the corresponding

---

44 See: J. Claessen, J. Blad, G.J. Slump et al., *Legislative Proposal to Introduce Provisions Governing Restorative Justice Services into the Dutch Code of Criminal Procedure and Explanatory Memorandum*, Oisterwijk: Wolf Legal Publishers, 2018; Claessen & Roelofs 2020; J. Claessen & G.J. Slump, 'De invoering van de voorwaardelijke eindezaakverklaring als mogelijke einduitspraak in het kader van mediation in strafzaken', *Tijdschrift voor Herstelrecht* 2022, 1, p. 94-99.

45 D. Johns, 'The Role of Community in Restorative Justice Conferencing', *Occasional Series in Criminal Justice and International Studies* 2008, p. 58-70, p. 61-62.

46 Ch. Pépin, *De ontmoeting. Een filosofie*, Gorredijk: Noordboek Filosofie, 2022, p. 74.

47 Pépin 2022, p. 24.

48 Pépin 2022, p. 83. Pépin is strongly influenced by the ideas of the Israeli-Jewish philosopher Martin Buber and the ideas of the French-Jewish philosopher Emmanuel Levinas. See: F. Hartensveld, *De mystiek van de ontmoeting. De betekenis van het dialogisch principe in het denken van Martin Buber*, Baarn: Gooi & Sticht, 1993; J. Keij, *De filosofie van Emmanuel Levinas. In haar samenhang verklaard voor iedereen*, Kampen: Uitgeverij Klement, 2009.

involvement with the other. Offenders and victims become people, vulnerable fellow human beings. Pépin writes:

> 'If you dare to make yourself vulnerable, you can free yourself at once from all the roles and attitudes that may get in the way of the encounter. (...) Making yourself vulnerable gives the other permission to do the same. (...) [B]y dropping my mask for [the other], I appeal to his sense of responsibility. I ask him to take care of me.'[49]

Once the encounter takes place, Pépin continues, 'it is no longer about what I am or am not going to achieve, but what we are going to achieve together'.[50] In the context of restorative justice, this means that the encounter enables an intersubjective conflict resolution, which will be perceived by parties as more just than the top-down dictated 'objective' judgment of a third party. Moreover, this intersubjective conflict resolution will be more constructive in nature than if people remain stuck in their friend-enemy mindset, as is often the case in a legal process.[51]

The horizontalization and democratization of restorative justice provisions such as mediation and the restorative conference should of course take place under certain conditions. These include the voluntariness (better: informed consent) of the parties, the acceptance of responsibility by the offender, the commitment of the

---

49 Pépin 2022, p. 143, 150 en 153.
50 Pépin 2022, p. 46. On the concept of 'participatory consciousness', see in this context: D. Bohm, *Over dialoog. Helder denken en communiceren*, Utrecht: Ten Have, 2020, especially p. 137-151.
51 The intersubjective nature of restorative justice provisions – also in terms of moral communication – is closely aligned with the assensus model described by Bianchi. See: Bianchi 1985, p. 88-92; H. Bianchi, *Basismodellen in de kriminologie*, Deventer: Van Loghum Slaterus, 1980, chapter 11.

parties to work it out together, the confidentiality and therefore open atmosphere between the parties as well as the supervision of the restoration process by a qualified mediator or facilitator. These conditions as well as the mediation or restorative conference itself can, to some extent, ensure that the Golden Rule in terms of distributive justice is respected. Moreover, in my view, they give substance to the Golden Rule in terms of procedural justice, since the conditions as well as the mediation or restoration conference itself symbolize autonomy and self-determination of parties, guidance and support for parties where needed as well as trust in parties to be able to resolve conflicts themselves. In short, people are treated well because they are not treated as passive objects but as active subjects.[52]

Room for punishment for the purpose of prevention?

Misdaadrecht (criminal law) – to use a term introduced by the Dutch criminologist Herman Bianchi[53] – is maturing, when intentionally harming the offender has become a last resort (*ultimum remedium*)[54] and when it offers room for people to solve their conflict themselves. Nevertheless, in my view, there is and remains room for punishment, when restorative justice fails to prevent new harm in the case of a

---

52 Hart 2020, p. 92-97.
53 H. Bianchi, 'Herstelrecht versus strafrecht', *Festus* 2010, 2, p. 18-22. The term *misdaadrecht* was introduced by the Dutch legal scholar Gerard van Hamel. In Dutch we normally use the term 'penal law' (*strafrecht*). Unlike criminal law, penal law is not a neutral term, because it has already been established what the reaction to crime should be, namely a punitive sanction, a penalty or a punishment. Criminal law (*misdaadrecht*), on the other hand, is originally a neutral term, since it does not say what the response to crime should look like. However, in daily practice, the term criminal law has obtained the meaning of penal law.
54 On the principle of subsidiarity, see: J. Blad, 'Herstelrecht en subsidiariteit van strafrecht, Een pleidooi voor herstelrecht als operationalisering van subsidiariteit', *Tijdschrift voor Herstelrecht* 2020, 2, p. 14-29; Claessen 2020.

specific offender. The question is whether punishment for the purpose of prevention should lead to a positive effect on a deeper level than the level of refraining from criminal behaviour out of fear of punishment (deterrence). The ideas of two philosophers are relevant here. First, those of Plato, whom we encountered earlier. According to Plato, no one commits a crime willingly. By this he means that only people who are damaged and confused commit crimes; the bad, the mad and the sad are, from this perspective, hardly distinguishable offender categories. The aim of the response to crime should always be 'the reform of the criminal's soul' or 'the cure of his mental and moral disease', and to this end punishment may be the appropriate means, according to Plato.[55] The French philosopher Simone Weil has a similar vision, when she writes: '[T]he art of punishment is the art of arousing in the criminal a desire for the pure good through pain (...).' However, Weil recognizes that we have lost 'any notion of punishment' because we no longer realize that 'it serves to provide the good'. 'For us, it stops at serving evil. That is why in our society something even more heinous exists than crime, and that is repressive justice', according to Weil.[56] Both philosophers consider punishment justified when it brings about an inner change in the sense that 'the love of good' is awakened in the offender. Damage and confusion then make way for healing and insight. With Plato and Weil, punishment clearly has a purpose beyond deterrence. While I appreciate their view, I nevertheless have to agree with Weil that punishment is in fact aimed at little else than retribution and

55 T.J. Saunders, *Plato's Penal Code. Tradition, Controversy, and Reform in Greek Penology*, Oxford: Clarendon Press, 2002, p. 1 and 351. Similarly, with the proviso that both authors consider punishment inappropriate: Sri Nisargadatta Maharaj, *Ik ben. Zijn*, Haarlem: Altamira-Becht, 2004; Mahatma Gandhi, *The Essential Writings*, Oxford: Oxford University Press, 2008.

56 S. Weil, *Waar strijden we voor? Over de noodzaak van anders denken*, Utrecht: Uitgeverij IJzer, 2021, p. 52-53.

deterrence. I can agree with punishment as a means of deterrence, but only as a last resort to prevent an offender from causing further harm to both others and themselves.

The view of mankind and the world behind restorative justice
As I move towards the end of my inaugural address, I want to say something about the view of man and the world behind restorative justice and, in particular, its implications. The American criminologist Howard Zehr writes:

> 'Underlying [restorative justice] is an assumption about society, namely that we are all connected (...) in a web of relationships. In this worldview, the problem of crime (...) is that it (...) represents a tear in the web of relationships. (...) In fact, damaged relationships are both cause and consequence of crime. (...) Mutual relationships imply mutual obligations and responsibilities.'[57]

From this perspective, the view of mankind and the world behind restorative justice is identical to the one behind the Golden Rule: 'To be is to be related.'[58] It is the last sentence in Zehr's quote that I want to elaborate on: 'Mutual relationships imply reciprocal obligations and responsibilities.' the question is whether these mutual obligations and responsibilities are now really being realized in the legal domain. It does not seem so. The Belgian pedagogue Wielemans states in this regard:

---

57 H. Zehr, *The Little Book of Restorative Justice. Revised & Updated*, New York: Good Books, 2015, p. 31.
58 Wielemans 1993, p. 1.

'At the legal level, responsibility is usually limited to that of the individual (...). Interpersonal influence (...) [is] rarely (...) sanctioned. (...) The administration of justice still predominantly operates with an unproblematized and very simplistic concept of the individual, and still to a large extent uses a Cartesian egocentric view of mankind.'[59]

This criticism affects not only criminal law but also restorative justice, especially if the latter were to focus exclusively on the offender's responsibility to make good what they have broken. In his definition of restorative justice, Zehr emphasises three concepts, namely: harms, needs and obligations.[60] What I am concerned with here are needs and obligations – rather: responsibilities. Needs obviously involve the needs of the victim. But they should also include the needs of the community as well as the needs of the offender. Responsibilities obviously include the responsibility of the offender to restore the harm caused by their crime. But it should also include the community's responsibility to treat both offenders and victims well. And it should also involve the victim's responsibility to show some good will towards the offender. A crime has many conscious and unconscious, direct and indirect causes and therefore guilt is a complicated concept, even if one does not completely dismiss the idea of free will.[61] Just as one speaks of primary victims (the direct victim), secondary victims

---

59 Wielemans 1993, p. 27.
60 Zehr 2015, p. 31 and 50.
61 J. Verplaetse, *Zonder vrije wil. Een filosofisch essay over verantwoordelijkheid*, Amsterdam: Nieuwezijds, 2011; J. Verplaetse, 'Van vergelden naar herstellen. De neuropsychologie van mediation in strafzaken', in: J. Claessen & A. van Hoek (red.), *Herstelrecht door de ogen van... Reflecties op restorative justice vanuit 27 verschillende perspectieven*, Den Haag: Boom criminologie, 2022, p. 117-138.

(family, friends) and tertiary victims (the community, the government), one can speak of primary offenders (the direct offender), secondary offenders (family, friends) and tertiary offenders (the community, the government). Viewed this way, when a crime is committed, everyone is a victim and an offender at the same time. For the time being, this vision is not socially acceptable. For this to happen, the integral worldview needs to break through on a larger scale. The restorative justice provision that can give expression to this vision is the restorative conference, in which not only the offender and the victim, but also their family and friends and the community participate. It is for good reason that the restorative conference is considered by some restorative justice thinkers to be the most complete restorative justice provision.[62] Pre-eminently, the restorative conference represents the public dimension of crime, which allows a restorative plan drawn up by all parties to replace punishment in principle.[63] Meanwhile, I am involved in a project in the Dutch province of Limburg (of which Maastricht is the capital city) that is aimed at the use of the restorative conference in tackling crime. It is precisely a restorative conference that makes it possible to expose causes of crime not only at the microlevel, but also at the meso- and macrolevel.

---

62 P. McCold & T. Wachtel, *In Pursuit of Paradigm: A Theory of Restorative Justice*, 2003.
63 In the Anglo-Saxon world, this is already happening in abundance, such as in New Zealand and Australia, where the judge approves a restoration plan drawn up by all parties in about 90% of the cases. See, among others: A. MacRae & H. Zehr, 'The Little Book of Family Group Conferences – New Zealand Style', in: H. Zehr et al., *The Big Book of Restorative Justice*, New York: Good Books, 2015, p. 203-280; K. Pranis, 'The Little Book of Circle Processes', in: Zehr et al. 2015, p. 281-358.

Between ideal and reality

Our crime approach has long been strongly focused on deterrence and incapacitation, using retribution as an instrument to maximize deterrence and incapacitation.[64] The aim of this approach is to influence offenders' behaviour through extrinsic discipline. The danger of offenders becoming objects is real in this way. So is the creation of enemy images and the declaration of war on them.[65] This approach, that only further fuels the illusion of separateness, needs to be readjusted by an approach that focuses both on the human being as a hub of relationships and on the person-to-person encounter. In other words, the extrinsically disciplining approach needs to be readjusted by an intrinsically motivating one, fuelled by the subjective and intersubjective domain. I see an important role here not only for *meditation*, but also for *mediation*.[66] Restorative justice is a relational vision of law *pur sang*, expressing not only the values of autonomy and equality, but also of brotherhood.[67] This is a truly enlightened vision of law, which is both distributively and procedurally consistent with the Golden Rule.

---

64 J. Claessen, 'Herstelrecht: een humaan alternatief voor het strafrecht – met Bijbelse inspiratie', in: S. van den Akker, A. de Haas, F. de Jong & T. de Roos (red.), *Opstellen over menselijkheid in het strafrecht*, Den Haag: Boom juridisch, 2022, p. 113-132.

65 Gibbs, Giever & Pober 2000, p. 119.

66 On the merging of meditation and mediation in the form of a 'meditative dialogue' or 'interpersonal meditation', see: G. Kramer, *Insight Dialogue. Een boeddhistische beoefening van meditatie in dialoog*, Rotterdam: Asoka, 2014, especially p. 18-19. On the lack of attention to the relational aspect in Zen Buddhism, see: Lathouwers 2019, p. 193-206.

67 C. Kelk, 'Vergelding, humanisering en herstel', in: J. Claessen & A. van Hoek (red.), *Herstelrecht door de ogen van… Reflecties op restorative justice vanuit 27 verschillende perspectieven*, Den Haag: Boom criminologie, 2022, p. 325-346.

I am aware that the current crime approach is often far and sometimes very far removed from restorative justice and the Golden Rule. It is therefore important to distinguish between ideal and reality. My ideal consists of a criminal law that humanely works on the restoration and prevention of harm. The reality, however, is a criminal law that starts from retribution or proportional revenge – which only leads to more harm. After all, by harming the offender, the harm to the victim and the community does not disappear. At most, it creates a new balance of power – and perhaps perverse delight (*Schadenfreude*), the worst of all sins according to Schopenhauer.[68] Moreover, answering violence with violence often only leads to more violence.[69] A society that punishes offenders with the aim of retribution or proportional revenge is ultimately no less damaged and confused than the offenders of crime themselves. However harsh reality may be, my compass remains focused on the ideal, and I see any movement towards it as progress. It is important, however, that this progression takes place from within people themselves – bottom-up, in other words. This requires that more and more people start living from the integral world view. Emancipation or becoming mature ultimately means nothing less than becoming like the father, who makes the sun rise on good and bad people and who makes it rain on the righteous and the unrighteous. For me, the most beautiful image of this universal and unconditional love is that of Kuan Yin, the female figure of compassion in Buddhism. The Dutch Zen teacher Ton Lathouwers writes about Kuan Yin: 'She is always mild and full of compassion, also for those who deserve a severe lesson before being saved. (...) She is (...) truly free from (...) vengefulness and [shows] aversion (...)

---

68 Schopenhauer 2010, especially p. 107.
69 Katie & Mitchell 2007, p. 101; Bianchi 1985, p. 88.

to any form of punishment.'[70] The *art* is to put Kuan Yin's compassion into practice yourself. It is the *art* of practising the Golden Rule and – by extension – restorative justice. It is the *art* of 'not taking sides' and 'receiving everything with open arms',[71] of moving beyond the duality between good and evil, but at the same time continuing the fight against evil from this new perspective.[72] Seen from this perspective, there are no monsters or devils, only human beings who are damaged and confused and who suffer because of this and who want to be liberated.[73] We together have the responsibility to bring back home those who are lost;[74] no one falls outside Indra's net.[75]

Closing remarks

In my inaugural address, I focused on a restorative *crime* approach. After all, I am a member of the Department of Criminal Law and Criminology. However, only a small part of all injustice is elevated into crime. Fortunately, restorative justice can also play a role outside criminal law, such as in private, administrative and disciplinary law. Restorative justice can also be applied in the civil society – for example, in the form of neighbourhood mediation, peaceful neighbourhoods and restorative cities. Moreover, interesting projects are currently emerging at the intersection of law and civil society under the denominator of 'socially effective justice', such as neighbourhood courts, youth courts in schools, houses of justice, justice in

---

70 Cited in: Lathouwers 2019, p. 110.
71 Katie & Mitchell 2007, p. 32.
72 Lathouwers 2019, p. 19.
73 Katie & Mitchell 2007, p. 32.
74 Lu 2019, p. 139.
75 T. Lathouwers, *Je kunt er niet uit vallen. Zentoespraken*, Rotterdam: Asoka, 2021, p. 26-27.

the bus or the neighbourhood, the juge de paix *et cetera*. Restorative justice principles also operate in these projects.

In my inaugural address, I also focused on a restorative approach to crime against *human beings*. However, the Golden Rule and the underlying view of man and the world invite restorative justice to go beyond anthropocentrism. It was Mencius, a Chinese philosopher from the fourth century BC, who emphasized that the Golden Rule applies not only to our fellow human beings, but to 'the ten thousand things', all that is – animals, trees, rivers *et cetera*.[76]

In short: restorative justice is starting to become reality, but there is still much work and research to be done and, above all, much patience to be exercised.

Acknowledgements
It is time to thank people. I now know how important person-to-person encounters are in life. In the words of the Israeli-Jewish philosopher Martin Buber: 'All real living is meeting.'[77] In recent years, I have had the opportunity to meet many people, for which I am grateful. I would like to mention a few 'junctions of relationships' explicitly to say thank you. First of all, the board members of the Restorative Justice Netherlands Foundation, the board members of the Bianchi Restorative Justice Foundation, the members of Maastricht University's Executive Board, the members of the Faculty Board and the members of the Department of Criminal Law and Criminology, who made the establishment of this endowed chair

---

76 Armstrong 2022, p. 50. See in this context also: K. van der Wal, 'Van sociale rechtsstaat naar ecologische rechtsstaat', in: J. Claessen & A. van Hoek (red.), *Herstelrecht door de ogen van... Reflecties op restorative justice vanuit 27 verschillende perspectieven*, Den Haag: Boom criminologie, 2022, p. 309-324.

77 Cited in: Loy 1993, p. 497; Pépin 2022, p. 157.

possible. You have ensured that from now on, research and educa-
tion in and from Maastricht will pay attention to restorative justice,
and that for once a legal scholar – and not a criminologist – sits on
this restorative justice chair.

Next year, I will have been working in the Department of Criminal
Law and Criminology at Maastricht University for twenty years:
the same place where I studied. Flying out is apparently not for me.
For that, I love my city and the people who live, work and/or just
enjoy life there too much. As the German philosopher Immanuel
Kant once said: 'You don't have to leave your own city to know the
world'. And that is true: the world is also present in Maastricht.
I can only say that I am still having a great time here and that I have
enjoyed working with you, colleagues and students, all these years.
Many thanks for that.

Furthermore, I would like to thank the people within the restorative justice community for inspiring me and building together
the road to restoration – both in theory and in practice. In the end,
it is neither about the goal nor the path, but the company. I got to
know most of you after my PhD – including Gert Jan Slump, Kim
Roelofs, Anneke van Hoek and Makiri Mual. Not only do I appreciate you for your work and our cooperation, but now I also consider
you my friends. A special word of thanks to my two great sources
of inspiration from the Low Countries: John Blad and Lode Walgrave. I consider it a privilege to be able to continue along the path
of restorative justice shaped by you. The name of Herman Bianchi
should not go unmentioned either. I am grateful to have known
this restorative justice pioneer for the last ten years of his life. Peter
Bal, a close colleague who passed away just before my promotion to
doctor, once called me 'the premature reincarnation of Bianchi'. I
take it as a compliment. Indeed, I still consider Bianchi my greatest

source of inspiration, who managed to bring together the worlds of law, linguistics, history, philosophy and religion.

Gratefully and with respect, I wear today the gown of our recently deceased former colleague Grat van den Heuvel. Grat was endowed professor of criminology in our department and had a keen interest in restorative justice. By wearing his gown, criminology and law meet again in Maastricht.

I now come to the most intimate circle of people I have had the pleasure of meeting. That circle consists first of all of family members present here in the room, Lilian and Erika, as well as family members connected at home via the livestream. Furthermore, that circle consists of old friends, including Dorris, Fleur, Marscha, Yvonne and Liam, and new friends, including Mirjam and Ruud. And then not only a word of thanks, but especially a word of love for my parents. Dad and mum, I am incredibly happy that we can celebrate this day together. And although you are averse to pride, I say to you: you can be a bit proud. But most of all, be happy and joyful. And finally, my dear Marc. You have been my buddy on my life journey for more than fifteen years now. You are my mirror, you show me that things can be done differently, but you give me the space to do the things my way – and, if necessary, you help me, because you have every confidence in me. Autonomy in connectedness. For me, that is the ultimate form of love. Thank you. I love you.

I have spoken.

Curriculum vitae

Prof. dr. Jacques Claessen (Maastricht, 1980) is endowed professor of restorative justice (RJN chair) and associate professor of criminal law in the Department of Criminal Law and Criminology of the Faculty of Law of Maastricht University. He is also guest lecturer at the Anton de Kom University of Suriname, deputy judge at the criminal law section of the Limburg District Court and co-editor-in-chief of the Dutch-Flemish Journal of Restorative Justice (*Tijdschrift voor Herstelrecht*). In 2012, he was the first to win the Bianchi Restorative Justice Prize – for his dissertation.[78] Since then, he has authored many publications on criminal sanctions and restorative justice – often from a meta-legal perspective – and is considered an expert on restorative justice in the Netherlands.

E-mail: jacques.claessen@maastrichtuniversity.nl

---

78   J.A.A.C. Claessen, *Misdaad en straf. Een herbezinning op het strafrecht vanuit mystiek perspectief* (diss. Maastricht), Nijmegen: Wolf Legal Publishers, 2010.